THE
HOUSEPLANT
LIBRARY

PLANTS FOR
SHADY
CORNERS

Kenneth A. Beckett

Salem House

First published in the United States by
Salem House Publishers, 1989, 462 Boston Street,
Topsfield, Massachusetts, 01983.

Text and photographs copyright © Kenneth A. Beckett 1989

Copyright © Swallow Publishing Ltd 1989

Conceived and produced by
Swallow Books, 260 Pentonville Road,
London N1 9JY

ISBN: 0 88162 383 0
Art Director: Elaine Partington
Editor: Catherine Tilley
Designers: Jean Hoyes and Hilary Krag
Studio: Del & Co
Typesetters: Bournetype, Bournemouth
Printed in Italy by Imago Publishing Limited

Author's acknowledgments

The great majority of pictures in this book are of plants
growing in botanical and private gardens. My wife Gillian,
who took most of the colour transparencies, and I are
particularly grateful to the following people for their
cooperation in allowing us access to their plant
collections behind the scenes: Mr C. D. Brickell, formerly
Director of the RHS Gardens, Wisley, Dr R. D. Shaw,
Curator of the Royal Botanic Garden, Edinburgh and
Mr J. B. E. Simmons, Curator of the Royal Botanic
Gardens, Kew. We are especially indebted to
Mr L. Maurice Mason for allowing us unlimited time
among his treasures at Talbot Manor, Fincham, Norfolk
over the years. As a result, more of his plants feature in
this book than anyone else's.

INTRODUCTION

Even the beginner to houseplant care appreciates the importance of light to green growing things. Without it, the essential chlorophyll cannot function and the plant turns yellow, becomes thin and weak and dies. Plants vary greatly in the amount of light they require, some must have direct sunlight, others will thrive in deep shade where the sun's surface is not seen from one year's end to the next.

The human eye is easily deceived by the apparent brightness of light in the home. When the sun shines through a window it seems very bright, but this is only in contrast to the lack of another light source. Window glass does, in fact, filter out the ultraviolet rays and greatly reduces the overall intensity the further one moves into the room. For this reason, comparatively few plants will enjoy being away from a window for long. Neither will many survive in a room lit solely by a north-facing window, or one shaded by a building so that it never receives direct sunlight.

All the plants described in this book will grow without direct sunlight, though some will be more successful if given the diffused but bright light of a north window, or behind a curtain in an east-, west- or south-facing one. For really dark corners it may be worth the modest expense of obtaining a custom-made artificial light unit, which will give enough illumination for the less light demanding plants to grow successfully without ever seeing natural daylight.

Siting, choosing and buying

If a plant is to be successful in the home it must be suitable for the position you have in mind. A plant that needs warmth will never be successful in a cool room. Basic information on the temperature and watering requirements of the plants described here are given in the easily understood symbols at the beginning of each entry.

The quality of houseplants for sale is mainly very good, whether purchased from a garden centre, nursery or multiple store. Nevertheless, avoid plants that look pale or have limp, flecked or crippled leaves. If the plants have flowers or buds, make sure they do not fall readily when the plant is gently shaken. In wintertime, bring the plant home as soon as possible, as prolonged chilling can result in partial withering or falling of leaves and flowers.

Watering

Applying too much or too little water to a containerized plant is the most common cause of root failure and death. For the beginner, deciding when to water a pot plant can be very difficult. As a rule, aim to keep the soil moist but not wet. Too much water will result in a sour, sodden soil ideal for root rot diseases, too little can produce a slow-growing plant with small leaves and flowers very prone to wilt or being prematurely shed. The easiest way to decide when a plant needs water is to probe into the soil surface to a depth of about 1cm (½in) with your finger tip. If the soil feels dry or barely damp, then give the plant a thorough watering by filling up the gap between the soil surface and the pot rim. If the plant is a cactus or a succulent, the soil should be allowed to dry out almost totally between waterings, and little or no water at all should be given between mid-autumn and mid-spring. Water orchids also in this way, but continue throughout the year.

Humidity

Many of the plants described here originate from areas of high rainfall where the air is humid, particularly during the growing season. Although many of these are remarkably tolerant of the dry air in many homes, most plants, especially ferns and orchids, will be healthier in moister air. Humidity can be increased by plunging the plant pots into deep trays of moist peat. Alternatively, the pots can be placed on flooded trays of gravel, as long as the water surface is kept below the pot bases. A third method is to use a fine droplet (mist) sprayer to wet the leaves at least once a day except when temperatures drop below the average minimum.

Feeding

Eventually the nutrients in potting soil of a plant run out and growth slows to a standstill, the lower leaves fall and all the young ones mature considerably smaller than is normal, and are often pale, or red, or purple-tinged. Before the plant reaches this extreme state of starvation, you should have begun feeding by applying one of the formulated liquid feeds easily available in garden centres. For a quick tonic, you could use foliar feeds, which contain highly soluble fertilizers and a wetting agent to be mixed with water and sprayed onto the foliage.

Top dressing

Plants kept for a long time in the same container should be top dressed every spring. To do this, use a small hand fork or a large kitchen fork to strip away the top layer of soil and fine roots, removing about one-sixth to one-quarter of the total depth of the root ball without damaging the larger roots. Replace the discarded layer with fresh soil containing, ideally, a granular, slow-release, general fertilizer. Finally, firm and water.

Pruning

Perennials, shrubs and climbers tend to become too large and need cutting back from time to time. Climbers and shrubs are best thinned out when dormant or after flowering in order to let in light and air. This can be best achieved by cutting out whole stems or branches to their bases or to ground level. The remaining growth can be shortened by one-quarter to one-third. Evergreen perennials, such as *Strobilanthes*, can be treated similarly except that the remaining stems should be cut back by a half or more. Deciduous or semi-deciduous perennials, for example *Achimenes* and *Hedychium*, need to be cut back to ground level as their foliage yellows.

How to use this book

This book contains a selection of the most suitable and readily available plants for shady corners, together with descriptions of the plants in their mature state, and their requirements (temperature, watering, and so on). These are given in the symbols, which are explained below. From this, you should be able to select a plant that meets your requirements exactly, and that will thrive in your home or conservatory. Although, as far as possible, technical terms have not been used in the main text of the book, there have been occasions when it has been impossible to avoid them. They are all explained in full in the glossary on page 63.

Symbol key

Cultural requirements and overall plant shape/growth habit are summarized in the form of at-a-glance symbols beside each entry. These provide quick reference and supplement the main description of the plant.

Temperature requirements

🌡 Tropical/warm – minimum 15–18°C (60–65°F)

🌡 Temperate – minimum 10–15°C (50–60°F)

🌡 Cool – minimum 5–10°C (40–50°F); down to –3°C (27°F) if noted as hardy

Watering requirements

Light – Allow rooting medium to dry out completely between waterings.

Medium – Allow surface of rooting medium to dry out between waterings.

Heavy – Keep entire rooting medium moist at all times.

Plant habit/shape

Erect

Spreading/prostrate

Mat-forming

Bushy

Weeping

Climbing/Scrambling

Rosette-forming

Pendent/Trailing

Tufted/Fan-like/Clump-forming

Globular (or cylindrical)

ACHIMENES
Gesneriaceae
Hot water plants

Origin: *Tropical areas of America (Mexico unless stated). A genus of 50 species of herbaceous perennials growing from small cone-like rhizomes made up of a mass of closely packed, fleshy scale leaves. They are sometimes incorrectly referred to as tubers. These rhizomes are usually bought dry, or stored in this way in winter and started into growth in spring. The spreading species and cultivars make good hanging basket plants. In pots, some form of support is necessary and twiggy sticks are satisfactory. The name 'hot water plant' probably came from instructions not to water them with cold water as they come from tropical climates, and in the days of irregularly heated houses they were difficult to grow. With modern heating they are easy and rewarding. The vivid, tubular or bell-shaped flowers open freely in summer. Propagate by natural increase of rhizomes.* Achimenes *is probably derived from the Greek word* achaemenis, *a magic plant.*

Below Achimenes cettoana
Bottom Achimenes 'Schneewitschen'

Species cultivated
A. cettoana
A bushy, erect species growing to 30cm (1ft) tall with whorls of narrowly lance-shaped 7cm (2¾in) long leaves. Flowers are tubular with spreading lobes, in shades from light to dark violet with a small white eye; they are 2.5cm (1in) long and 12mm (½in) across.
A. longiflora Mexico southwards to Panama
A trailing plant with stems reaching 30cm (1ft) or more and leaves 8cm (3in) long. The large tubular flowers grow to 7cm (2¾in) across, varying in colour from lavender to dark purple-blue, with a white throat. *A.l. alba* is white with a few purple markings. 'Guerrero' is a pale violet-blue with wavy petal lobes; 'Major' has 8cm (3in) wide violet-blue flowers – the largest achimenes.

Cultivars
Many named cultivars have been raised by hybridizing the best of the species, their parentage often being uncertain or complex. A selection is listed alphabetically:
'Ambroise Verschaffelt', of trailing habit, the flowers white with strong purple veining.
'Elke Michelssen', a compact plant with purplish-pink flowers.
'Little Beauty', erect with crimson-pink flowers having a yellow eye.
'Paul Arnold', deep purple flowers with a white throat which is marked with yellow and purple.
'Peach Blossom', a trailing plant with magenta-pink flowers.
'Pink Beauty', spreading with pale crimson-pink flowers.
'Purple King' ('Pulcherrima', 'Patens Major'), a compact plant up to

38cm (15in) with rich, reddish-purple flowers.

'Schneewitschen', a spreading plant with long-tubed, pure white flowers.

'Yellow Beauty', erect with primrose-yellow flowers; the first really yellow-flowered achimenes hybrid.

ADIANTUM
Adiantaceae
Maidenhair ferns

Origin: *Cosmopolitan, especially tropical America. A genus of 200 species of evergreen and deciduous ferns. They are generally typified by blackish glossy leaf stalks (stipes) and leaves which are cut into several deep, narrow lobes and can be pinnate, bipinnate or multipinnate. The individual leaflets (pinnae or pinnules) vary from oblong to triangular to fan shaped, occasionally rounded and usually lobed. The spore clusters (sori) are borne on the edges of the pinnae. Plants require shade from direct sun at all times of the year. Propagate either by division or by sowing spores in spring. Some species are tufted, others grow from rhizomes; all are among the best ferns for the home.* Adiantum *comes from the Greek* adiantos, *dry or unwetted, alluding to the water-repellent surface of the fronds, most species being very resistant to dry air.*

Species cultivated

A. raddianum (*A. cuneatum, A. aemulum*) Tropical America

A tufted species with the blade of the frond roughly triangular, 15–30cm (6–12in) long, two- to four-pinnate. The pinnules are

Adiantum raddianum
'Fritz Luthi'

diamond-shaped to oblong, about 7mm (¼in) long. This is an enormously variable species giving rise to most of the commonly grown tender maidenhairs. These include (all tropical):

'Brilliant Else', like 'Elegantissimum' but the young fronds are light red.

'Decorum', much like true A. *raddianum*, but more robust with thicker frond stalks and broader, blunter pinnules.

'Double Leaflet', pinnules cleft into two to four tiny pinnule-like narrow segments, creating highly ornamental, mist-like foliage.

'Elegantissimum', drooping pale green fronds, the pinnules growing to 4mm ($\frac{3}{16}$in), fan-shaped.

'Fragrantissimum' ('Fragrans' in some catalogues), larger than the true species and more vigorous, with pinnules growing to 1.5cm ($\frac{5}{8}$in) long.

'Fritz Luthi', neat, lacy fronds, the 1cm ($\frac{3}{8}$in) pinnules carried at various angles.

'Gracillimum', pinnules variable but only 2–4mm ($\frac{1}{16}$–$\frac{3}{16}$in) long, rarely larger. A very elegant cultivar.

'Kensington Gem', a very robust cultivar with a total height of 1m (3ft). In all respects it is like a super *raddianum*, but sterile and possibly of hybrid origin.

'Pacific Maid', pinnae are large, up to 2cm (¾in) long, overlapping and forming a dense frond.

A. scutum See A. *tenerum*.

A. tenerum (A. *scutum*) Florida, West Indies, Mexico to Peru.
A tufted plant, with the blade of the fronds triangular to oval, three- to four-pinnate and 40–75cm (16–30in) long. Pinnules are rounded to diamond-shaped, 1–2cm (⅜–¾in) long and asymmetrical. Cultivars include (all tropical):

'Farleyense', mostly fan-shaped pinnules which are lobed and ruffled; they are up to 4cm (1½in) in length and overlap.

'Scutum', pinnules both larger and broader than the type.

'Scutum Roseum', similar to 'Scutum' but the young fronds are a reddish colour.

AECHMEA
Bromeliaceae

Origin: *West Indies and South America. A genus of 150 mainly epiphytic species (that is, in the wild they grow perched on another plant) many of which make extremely durable pot plants. They are rosette-forming plants with sword-shaped, toothed or spiny, arching to erect leaves, the bases of which fit together forming a water-holding cup. The three-petalled flowers are carried in spike-like panicles, usually on long stems, often bearing coloured bract leaves. The berry-like fruits can be brightly coloured. After blooming the rosette*

slowly dies as young offsets form around the base. Propagate by offsets in late spring.

Aechmea *derives from the Greek* aichme, *a point, the sepals having rigid points.*

Above Aechmea
fasciata 'Variegata'
Above left Aechmea
fulgens discolor

Species cultivated

A. discolor See *A. fulgens discolor*
A.d. albiflora Flowers white.
A. fasciata (*Billbergia rhodocyanea*) Silver vase, Urn plant Brazil
A flowering plant up to 50cm (20in) in height. Leaves are broad, densely grey-scaled and usually banded with silvery-white. Plants with brightly marked leaves have been selected by nurserymen. Purple-blue flowers and pink bracts form a dense pyramid. *A.f.* 'Variegata' has creamy-yellow, longitudinal stripes.
A. fulgens Coralberry Brazil
A flowering plant up to 40–50cm (16–20in) in height. Leaves grow to 45cm (1½ft) and are grey green with some cross-banding. The long inflorescence, up to 20cm (8in), has violet purple flowers becoming red. Fruits are red.
A.f. discolor (*A. discolor*)
The undersides of leaves are dark red.

Aechmea × 'Foster's Favourite'

Hybrids

A. × 'Foster's Favorite' (*A. victoriana* × *racinae*)
Lacquered wine-cup
This popular hybrid is usually about 40cm (16in), but can reach up to 60cm (2ft) in height. The leaves are a striking wine red and the nodding spikes of red flowers are followed by red fruits, which make the plant a strikingly decorative subject all the year round.
A. 'Foster's Favorite Favorite'
A sport of 'Foster's Favorite', similar, but with the leaves bordered with a broad cream band and an overall red flush.

AGLAONEMA

Araceae
Chinese evergreens

Origin: *Tropical and sub-tropical S.E. Asia. A genus of 21 species of evergreen perennials. They are tufted plants, having short stems which give some species an almost shrubby appearance. The oval to oblong lance-shaped leaves are often patterned and the small petalless flowers are carried on a short spadix with an arum-like spathe. The bright red fruits are not often formed. Propagate by division or by summer cuttings. A genus of well-tried houseplants which actually thrive in poor light.* Aglaonema *derives from the Greek* aglaos, *bright and* nema, *a thread, referring to the stamens.*

Below *Aglaonema commutatum* 'Treubii'
Bottom *Aglaonema commutatum*

Species cultivated

A. commutatum Molucca islands
A very variable plant. Thick-textured, oblong lance-shaped leaves grow up to 25cm (10in) long, dark green with grey feathering. Greeny-white spathes are carried on 8cm (3in) stems.

A.c. pseudobracteatum
The stems are white with green marbling. The leaves are longer and narrower, with yellow and green mottling and distinct white veins. *A.c.* 'Malay Beauty' is a more robust form. *A.c.* 'Treubii' is smaller and neater, with bluish-green leaves marbled with silvery grey. *A.c.* 'Tricolor' has broadly elliptical leaves, variegated on both surfaces and carried on pinky-white leaf stalks.

Hybrids

'Silver Queen', oval leaves, overlaid with a paler green and silvery variegation which almost totally covers the leaf surfaces.

Alocasia × amazonica

ALOCASIA
Araceae

Origin: *Tropical Asia. A genus of 70 evergreen perennials growing from thick, fleshy rhizomes which can be erect and stem-like, or occasionally tuberous. The handsome leaves are arrowhead- to heart-shaped, sometimes deeply lobed and peltate, that is, having stalks which appear to join the leaf underneath rather than at the edge. Petalless flowers are borne on a spadix within an arum-like spathe, but are not decorative. Propagate by suckers, or cuttings of the rhizomes in spring.* Alocasia *derives from the Greek a, without, and* Colocasia, *a closely related genus from which species were removed to form Alocasia.*

Species cultivated
A. × amazonica (*A. sanderiana × A. lowii*)
Leaves are 30–40cm (12–16in) long, arrowhead-shaped, peltate, with a wavy edge, very dark, glossy green strikingly contrasting with wide white veins and a narrower white edge.

ALPINIA
Zingiberaceae

Origin: *Tropical and sub-tropical Asia and Polynesia. A genus of 250 handsome species of mainly evergreen perennials growing from rhizomes. They form clumps of erect stems clad with lance-shaped to*

Alpinia sanderae oval, undivided leaves. The inflorescence, which can be a raceme or panicle, is usually borne at the end of the stem, but in some cases is on a much shorter, leafless stem growing direct from the rhizome. Individual flowers are somewhat orchid-like in appearance and may or may not be sheltered by a colourful bract. Propagate by division in early summer. Alpinia *commemorates the Italian Prospero Alpino (1553–1616), Professor of Botany at Padua.*

Species cultivated

A. sanderae Variegated ginger New Guinea

Stems are clustered, slender and up to 45–60cm (1½–2ft) tall. Leaves are 20cm (8in) long, lustrous pale green, boldly striped and edged with pure white. It rarely, if ever, blooms as a pot plant. The status of this plant is uncertain, but it may be a dwarf, variegated form of *A. rafflesiana.*

ANTHURIUM

Araceae

Origin: *Humid rain forests of tropical America and the West Indies. A genus of evergreen perennials containing 550 species of which a number are grown for their decorative foliage and flowers. Some are low-growing and form tufts, others climb by aerial roots. The leathery leaves are usually lustrous dark green and can be prettily patterned. The flowers are small, grouped together in a spadix and arise from a flattened spathe which in some species is brightly coloured. This large*

genus contains many good houseplants. *Propagate by division or seed in spring.* Anthurium *derives from* anthos, *a flower, and* oura, *tail, from the shape of the spadix.*

Species cultivated

A. andreanum Tailflower Colombia
An erect plant with a short stem. Leaves are long-stalked, oblong and lobed to make a heart shape, 15–20cm (6–8in) long, leathery and dark green. The spathe is orange-red to scarlet, 10cm (4in) or more long with a rippled surface; the spadix is yellow. *A.a.* 'Album' has white spathes stained with purple at the base. *A.a.* 'Giganteum' has salmon-red spathes which are much larger than the type. *A.a.* 'Rubrum' has deep red spathes and white spadices with yellow tips.

A. crystallinum Crystal anthurium Peru, Colombia
The leaves are oval and lobed to make a heart shape, 25–38cm (10–15in) long, lustrous deep green, marked with a pattern of silver-white veins. Spathe is green, very narrowly oblong, 9cm (3½in) long, and not decorative. Plants with leaves smaller than given above may well be hybrids with the smaller but similar *A. forgetii.*

A. scherzerianum Flamingo flower Costa Rica
Leaves are erect, short-stalked, deep green, oblong and lance-shaped, growing up to 15cm (6in) or more in length. They set off the broadly oval 8cm (3in) long spathes, which are waxy and bright scarlet, contrasting with the yellow, spirally twisted spadix. Cultivars with darker red, white, pink and spotted spathes are grown.

Above Anthurium crystallinum **Top** Anthurium scherzerianum

Aspidistra elatior 'Variegata'

ASPIDISTRA
Liliaceae

Origin: *East Asia. A genus of eight species of evergreen perennials, having horizontal rhizomes and oval, parallel-veined green leaves held upright on long stalks. Their flowers are unusual in that they have their parts arranged in fours, as opposed to threes, which is normal for members of the lily family. Propagate by division. Aspidistras were very popular foliage houseplants in the nineteenth century, being especially tolerant of dust, fumes and general neglect; there was even a song written about them. They have stood the test of time and still make very durable plants for the home.* Aspidistra *derives from the Greek* aspidion, *a small round shield, referring to the rounded end of the large stigma.*

Species cultivated
A. elatior (*A. lurida*) Cast iron plant China
A clump-forming plant. Leaves are long-stalked, oblong lance-shaped, dark lustrous green, 45–75cm (1½–2½ft) long. Flowers are solitary, cup-shaped, purple and borne at ground level. *A.e.* 'Variegata' has leaves striped longitudinally with white.

ASPLENIUM

Aspleniaceae
Spleenworts

Origin: *World-wide from tropical to cool temperate zones. A genus of 650 species of perennial ferns that generally form tufts or short rhizomes. The elegant leaves are undivided and smooth-edged to tripinnatifid; their spore clusters (sori) are usually very narrow, though sometimes oval, and are borne along the veins on the undersides of the pinnae. Propagate by division or by spores in spring, or with some species by removing plantlets in summer. The species described is among the best ferns for use in the home.* Asplenium *derives from the Greek* a, *not and* splen, *the spleen, an allusion to its supposed medicinal properties in curing diseases of the spleen.*

Asplenium nidus

Species cultivated

A. nidus (A. *nidus-avis*) Bird's nest fern
Tropical Asia and Australia
This plant has fronds reaching 90cm (3ft) or more in length, which are lance-shaped, semi-erect, forming a broad, spreading funnel, rich shining green with a black mid-rib. Sori are very narrow. In the wild this species is epiphytic, and will tolerate drought conditions for short periods. Tropical.

BEGONIA

Begoniaceae

Origin: *Widely distributed in tropical to warm temperate climates, most frequent in South America, but almost absent from Australasia and the Pacific Islands. A genus of 900 mainly perennial species including some sub-shrubs and climbers. Although very variable, most have characteristic lop-sided, ear-shaped leaves often with beautiful markings. Flowers are of single sex, usually in clusters, with four to five (rarely two) tepals, the ovaries being winged or strongly angled. Some species are tufted and sub-shrubby with a fibrous root system, others grow from rhizomes or tubers. Propagate rhizomatous and tuberous species by division, or by leaf or stem cuttings, or by seed. Most species and hybrids in this huge genus make very good houseplants.* Begonia *was named for Michel Bégon (1638–1710), patron of botany and at one time Governor of French Canada.*

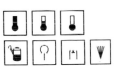

Species cultivated
B. rex Painted leaf/Fan begonia Assam
A rhizomatous plant. Leaves are broadly oval, the surface crinkly or puckered, dark green with a metallic sheen and a broad band edged

Begonia sutherlandii

with silver. Flowers are pink, growing in small, erect clusters. Very shade tolerant. Temperate. Most of the named cultivars are of hybrid origin. They have very ornamental and colourful leaves, usually with a dark centre and an edge separated by a whitish or silvery area. Colours can vary from pink, through reds, maroons and browns to all shades of green. These are among the most striking of all foliage begonias.

B. sutherlandii South Africa

A tuberous-rooted plant, growing to 15cm (6in) with slender, branched, hanging stems 30–60cm (1–2ft) long. Leaves are oval, up to 8–10cm (3–4in) or more in length, with shallow lobes, pale green with red veins. Flowers are orange and up to 2cm (¾in) across. An excellent species for a hanging basket. Temperate.

BERTOLONIA
Melastomataceae

Origin: *Brazil and Venezuela. A genus of ten species of evergreen perennials. They are small plants with decorative oval to heart-shaped or elliptic, somewhat fleshy leaves often patterned in white or silver or having a metallic, almost crystalline, lustre. The flowers, which are carried in clusters at the ends of the stems, are small and may be removed as soon as the spike appears. They are natives of tropical rain forests, where they grow on the ground and are thus adapted to a high humidity and no direct sunlight. In the home these conditions are best provided by a glass case or terrarium. Propagate by stem or*

leaf cuttings in a case with a minimum temperature of 21–23°C (70–74°F). Bertolonia *was named for Antonio Bertolini (1775–1869), Professor of Botany at Bologna.*

Species cultivated

B. marmorata

Leaves are oblong to oval and lobed, making a heart shape, 11–20cm (4½–8in) long, velvety green with depressed veins giving the leaf a quilted look, and a central silvery stripe; the undersides are purple. Flowers are small and red-purple. *B.m.* 'Mosaica' has broader silvery leaf vein marking with pinkish tints.

B.m. aenea

Leaves have a coppery or bronze lustre without the silvery marking.

Bertolonia marmorata

BILLBERGIA
Bromeliaceae

Origin: *Tropical and sub-tropical America. A genus of 50 species of evergreen perennials most of which in the wild grow perched on trees*

Billbergia × *windii*

(epiphytic), though a few grow naturally on the ground. They have leathery, strap-shaped leaves usually in a rosette, which is tubular and water-holding at the base. The rosettes can grow one to a stem but are normally clustered. Flowers are tubular, comprising three petals and often colourful, borne within showy bracts atop an arched or sometimes erect stem. Plants are tolerant of poor conditions and neglect but can become shabby and then are slow to recover. With their attractive flowers these bromeliads are rewarding house or conservatory plants. Propagate by division or offsets. Billbergia was named for J.G. Billberg (1772–1844), a Swedish botanist.

Species cultivated

B. nutans Queen's tears, Friendship plant Brazil, Argentina and Uruguay
Leaves are dark green, up to 40cm (16in) long, borne in tubular rosettes which can build up into dense clumps. The flowering stem is erect, arching at the tip; flowers are greenish-yellow edged with purple-blue and with pink bracts, opening in early spring. Nectar forms within the flowers and sometimes spills out when the plant is touched, giving rise to one of its common names.

B. pyramidalis Brazil
The leaves are broadly strap-shaped, up to about 30cm (1ft) long, finely toothed and carried in vase-shaped rosettes. Stem is erect, bearing red bracts and purple, crimson-tipped flowers in summer. *B.p.* 'Striata' (Striped urn plant) has dark green leaves striped with cream; winter flowering.

B. rhodocyanea See *Aechmea fasciata*.

B. × windii (*B. decora × B. nutans*)
The leaves are very narrow, grey-green, growing to a length of 30cm (1ft), slightly twisted, arching, forming shortly tubular rosettes soon making densely packed clumps. Flowers are greenish-yellow edged with purple-blue, together with large rose-red bracts, borne on strongly arching stems at intervals throughout the year.

BLECHNUM

Blechnaceae (Polypodiaceae)

Origin: World-wide, but chiefly in the southern hemisphere. A genus of 220 species of handsome decorative ferns, usually evergreen, but some are partly deciduous. They have pinnate or lobed fronds like an outspread palm, in most species forming rosettes but occasionally in tufts or spaced on rhizomes, forming mats. The spore clusters (sori) are linear and are found on either side of the midribs of the pinnae, sometimes on separate, fertile, erect fronds with narrower pinnae. Those cultivated under cover are chiefly tropical species and grow well in containers if given warmth and shade. They are also more

Blechnum gibbum

tolerant of drier atmospheres than many ferns. Propagate by division or by spores. Blechnum derives from the classical Greek name for an unknown species of fern and was adopted for this genus by Linnaeus.

Species cultivated

B. gibbum (*Lomaria gibba*) New Caledonia and adjacent islands Fronds are 60-90cm (2-3ft) long, lance-shaped to narrowly oval, the pinnae are very slender and tapering to a point. The narrower, fertile fronds are erect. The rosette is wide-spreading, topping a slender, black-scaly trunk reaching 90cm (3ft) in height. An elegant miniature tree fern.

B.g. platyptera
Somewhat larger and faster growing; it may be of hybrid origin.

CHIRITA

Gesneriaceae

Origin: *Indo-Malaysia, S.E. Asia and southern China. A genus of 80 species of evergreen perennials and annuals of varied appearance. Some species form rosettes, others produce erect leafy stems. A third group produces a short, erect stem topped by one very large leaf and a cluster of smaller ones. All species bear tubular flowers with five, usually rounded, petal lobes. The species described thrives in pots.*

Chirita sinensis   *Propagate by seed in late winter or spring and by cuttings in spring or summer. Chirita derives from the Nepalese common name for a gentian; some species have gentian-blue flowers.*

Species cultivated

C. sinensis China (including Hong Kong)

A rosette-forming plant. Leaves are stalked, oval to elliptic, 13–20cm (5–8in) long. The basic species has thick-textured, almost fleshy, rich green corrugated leaves, but silvery-white patterned forms occur in the wild and these are most commonly cultivated. Flowers are 3–4cm (1¼–1½in) long, the tube white marked with yellow, the lobes lilac to purple, usually in clusters on stems well above the leaves in summer. Must be grown in sharply drained soil and watered with care.

CHLOROPHYTUM

Liliaceae

Origin: Chiefly from Africa, but also in warmer parts of South America, Australia and Asia. A genus of 215 species of stemless perennials with short rhizomes and fleshy roots. Their leaves are very narrow or lance-shaped to oval with parallel veins. The flowers are starry with six tepals in loose racemes on slender, branched stems. Those cultivated are non-demanding plants for the house or conservatory. Propagate those which produce plantlets on their stems by detaching them when they have grown four to five leaves and then potting them singly. All species can also be propagated by seed if available, or by division. Chlorophytum derives from the Greek

chlorus, *green and* phytum, *a plant, an unremarkable description that could be used to apply to almost every genus.*

Species cultivated

C. bichetii See under *C. laxum.*

C. capense (*C. elatum, Anthericum elatum*) Spider plant South Africa

The leaves are 25–60cm (10–24in), pale green. Flowering stems are branched, growing up to 120cm (4ft). Flowers are 1.5–2cm (½–¾in) wide, in small clusters. Confused with, and sometimes considered a form of, *C. comosum. C.c.* 'Variegatum' has leaves with pale creamy-yellow, longitudinal stripes.

C. comosum (*Anthericum comosum*) Spider plant South Africa

Similar to *C. capense*, but with leaves only 20–45cm (8–18in) long, and flowering stems 30–60cm (1–2ft). Flowers are 2cm (¾in) or more wide, produced together with small plantlets, which weigh down the stems so that they hang. It is this characteristic that makes the spider plant such a good subject for a hanging basket. *C. capense* does not produce plantlets. *C.c.* 'Variegatum' has striped leaves.

C. elatum See *C. capense.*

C. laxum Tropical Africa

A tufted to clump-forming species. Leaves are very narrow to narrowly lance-shaped, 13–20cm (5–8in) long and arching. Flowers are 2cm (¾in) across, white, growing in slender spike-like panicles. *C.l.* 'Variegatum' (*C. bichetti*) has leaves edged and variably striped with cream

Chlorophytum laxum
'Variegatum'

Cissus antarctica

CISSUS
Vitidaceae

Origin: *Tropical and sub-tropical regions of the world. A genus of 34 species of climbing and succulent shrubs. They have woody or herbaceous stems with alternate leaves and most have tendrils. Flowers are small, usually greenish and four-petalled in branched clusters. They are followed by berry-like fruits. All species are suitable for the conservatory and nearly all, including C. antartica, are excellent houseplants. Cissus is derived from the Greek* kissos, *ivy, many species being woody climbers.*

Species cultivated

C. antarctica Kangaroo vine Australia

A vigorous woody climber, growing to 5m (16ft) or more in the wild, far less in a pot. Leaves are 7–15cm (2¾–6in), oval to oval-oblong, usually somewhat toothed, leathery and glossy, dark green above, paler beneath. Opposite each leaf is a forked tendril. The insignificant flowers are borne in small, axillary clusters. A very tolerant and popular houseplant.

CLIVIA

Amaryllidaceae

Origin: *Warm dry forests of South Africa. A genus containing three species of evergreen perennials. They are clump-forming, with dark green leathery, strap-shaped, arching leaves and six-tepalled, funnel-shaped flowers borne in umbels at the ends of the stems. Clivias make very good houseplants, but must be kept cool for a couple of months in late autumn to early winter to initiate flower buds. The roots are very thick and fleshy and plants are best left undisturbed until too large for their intended use, when they should be carefully divided. Apart from division, propagate by removing offsets when they have*

Clivia miniata

three or four leaves, or by seed (sown as soon as ripe). Clivia *was named for the Duchess of Northumberland, née Charlotte Florentina Clive (granddaughter of Robert Clive), in whose garden it first flowered in Great Britain.*

Species cultivated

C. miniata (*Imantophyllum miniatum*) Kaffir lily
The most attractive species with robust, thick-textured, strap-shaped leaves 40–60cm (16–24in) long and 2.5–5cm (1–2in) wide. Flowers are orange to red, 5–8cm (2–3in) long, broadly funnel-shaped, borne in rounded umbels of up to 20 or more blooms in spring and summer. *C.m.* 'Citrina' has yellow flowers. *C.m.* 'Striata' has variegated leaves.

C. nobilis (*Imantophyllum aitonii*)
Less vigorous than *C. miniata* with leaves 30–50cm (12–20in) long. Flowers are tubular, slightly curved and hanging up to 4cm (1½in) long, reddish with green tips, borne in umbels of up to 40, occasionally more, in late spring.

CODONANTHE

Gesneriaceae

Codonanthe gracilis

Origin: *Tropical America. A genus of 15 species of evergreen perennials, sub-shrubs and climbers that grow perched on trees (epiphytic). Some species make tolerant and pleasing houseplants – the one described here is an ideal hanging basket subject, having oval to elliptic leaves in pairs and smallish tubular flowers with five petal lobes in their axils. The berry-like fruits which follow may be brightly coloured and add to the plant's season of attraction. Propagate by cuttings in summer, or by seed in spring.* Codonanthe *derives from the Greek* kodon, *a bell and* anthos, *a flower, the tubular base of the blooms being somewhat bell-like, at least in some species.*

Species cultivated

C. gracilis Central America
Stems are prostrate or hanging, up to 30–60cm (1–2ft) long. Leaves are 2.5–4cm (1–1½in) long, elliptic to lance-shaped and slender-pointed. The flowers grow up to 2cm (¾in) long.

COLOCASIA

Araceae

Origin: *S.E. Asia to Polynesia. A genus of eight species of perennials that grow from rhizomes or tuberose roots, cultivated for their large long-stalked leaves, which rise in a cluster from ground level. Plants*

Colocasia esculenta

are best for a warm conservatory, but can be tried in the home where the atmosphere is not too dry. Colocasia derives from the Greek kolocasia, originally used for the rhizomes of the sacred lotus.

Species cultivated

C. esculenta (including *C. antiquorum*) Taro, Elephant's ear, Cocoyam, Dasheen S.E. Asia
Rarely reaching over 90cm (3ft) in a pot, this plant grows from a tuber-like, starchy corm. Leaves are 20–50cm (8–20in), deeply heart-shaped at the base. The spathe is pale yellow, 15–25cm (6–10in) long, but only borne on large plants. *C.e.* 'Illustris' has violet-brown leaves which have bright green veins.

CTENANTHE

Marantaceae

Origin: *Tropical South and Central America. A genus of 15 species of evergreen perennials classified by some botanists under* Myrosma, *some of which are grown for their handsome foliage. They have*

Ctenanthe oppenheimiana
'Tricolor'

usually narrowly oblong leaves which are undivided and smooth-edged and are similar in general appearance to Calathea. *The dense flower spikes bear closely overlapping, persistent bracts. Propagate by division in spring or summer.* Ctenanthe *is derived from the Greek* kteis *or* ktenos, *a comb and* anthos, *a flower, referring to the arrangement of the floral bracts.*

Species cultivated

C. oppenheimiana Brazil
A bushy shrub growing to 2m (6½ft) when mature. Leaves are lance-shaped, leathery, up to 30cm (1ft) or more long, dark green above with silvery-white bands following the lines of the veins on either side of the midribs, red beneath. *C.o.* 'Tricolor' (Never never plant) has the silvery variegation overlain with splashes of creamy-white and a lighter red beneath.

CYRTOMIUM

Aspidiaceae

Cyrtomium fortunei

Origin: *S.E. Asia and Polynesia. A genus of about ten species included by some botanists in the genus* Phanerophlebia. *They have densely scaly rhizomes and once-pinnate fronds with broad, asymmetrical leaflets which may or may not be toothed. Brown spore capsules with*

centrally fixed covering membranes are borne abundantly on the undersides of the fronds. They are very tolerant pot plants for the home or conservatory, succeeding well in a cold porch or a heated room. Propagate by division of multicrowned plants or by spores. Cyrtomium derives from the Greek kyrtos, *arched, with reference to the arching fronds.*

Species cultivated

C. falcatum (*Aspidium falcatum, Polystichum falcatum*) Holly fern
Asia from India to Korea and Japan, Hawaii and South Africa
A plant of tufted growth with 35–65cm (14–26in) long, arching fronds; these fronds are pinnate, with up to 23 oblong oval, wavy edged pinnae ending in a tail-like point, shining deep green above, the undersides softly brown-hairy with abundant spore clusters (sori) on fertile fronds.

C.f. rochfordianum
A stronger-growing species, with broader fronds having distinctly toothed and wavy edges.

C. fortunei (*Aspidium falcatum fortunei*) Japan, Korea and China
Basically like *C. falcatum*, but somewhat smaller in all its parts, with each frond composed of up to twice as many, less taper-pointed and less glossy leaflets. Suitable for unheated rooms.

DAVALLIA

Davalliaceae

Origin: *S.W. Europe, Canary Is., Malagasy and tropical and sub-tropical Pacific Islands and Asia as far north as Korea and Japan. A genus of 40 species of mainly small to medium sized ferns, which in the wild grow perched on trees (epiphytic). They are excellent plants for hanging baskets or can be grown on tree bark, moss sticks or in pans, being suitable for the conservatory or home, but it is necessary to provide extra humidity in warm weather. All species become dormant for at least a short time between autumn and late spring. Species from hot, dry places, such as D.* canariensis, *are dormant for four to six weeks in summer. Propagate by division, by rhizome sections taken as cuttings, or by spores. Davallia commemorates Edmond Davall (1763–98), a Swiss botanist and friend of James Edward Smith (1759–1828), founder of the Linnean Society of London, to whom he bequeathed his herbarium.*

Davallia canariensis

Species cultivated

D. canariensis Hare's foot fern Canary Is., Spain, N. Africa
With stout rhizomes appearing furry, densely covered with narrow, chaffy brown scales. Fronds are 25–45cm (10–18in) long, triangular, quadripinnatifid, deciduous in summer.

DICKSONIA
Dicksoniaceae

Dicksonia antartica

Origin: *Malaysia to Australasia, St. Helena, tropical America. A genus of 30 species of large ferns, most of which build up trunks with age. Their fronds are arching and bi- or tripinnate, giving an elegantly lacy effect, and they make very attractive foliage plants. Propagate by spores in spring at about 15°C(61°F). Dicksonia was named for James Dickson (1738–1832), a British nurseryman and botanist.*

Species cultivated

D. antarctica Soft tree fern Eastern Australia from Queensland to Tasmania

Stems eventually grow to 5m (16ft) tall in the open garden, covered with a rusty brown bark-like surface of matted roots. Young plants are stemless, the rosettes of fronds arising at ground level. Each frond is 1.3–3m (4½–9ft) long, tripinnate, the spore clusters (sori) at the ends of the veins near the edges of the leaflets, which bend back to cover them.

EPIPHYLLUM
Cactaceae

Origin: *Tropical South America to Mexico. A genus of 21 species of cacti which are epiphytic, that is, they grow perched on another plant. They are woody at the base when mature, the stems flattened and broadened until they resemble leaves. The flowers, which are trumpet-shaped and have many tepals, are large and showy. Some species open their blooms at night, others by day. They are excellent plants for the conservatory and home, in pots or in hanging baskets, but they must have a cool, dry rest in winter, though unlike most cacti they must never become totally dry. Propagate by cuttings, taking stem sections ('leaves') in summer, or by seed in spring.* Epiphyllum *derives from the Greek* epi, *upon and* phyllon, *a leaf, alluding to the way the flowers appear to grow from the leaf edges, which are in fact modified stems.*

Species cultivated
E. ackermannii (*Nopalxochia ackermannii*) Orchid cactus Mexico
Stems are 30–60cm (1–2ft) long, bearing tiny areoles with a few spines on their shallowly toothed edges. The crimson flowers grow to 15cm (6in) long. The true species is very rare in cultivation, its place being taken by a wide range of hybrids, for which see below.

Hybrids
These are hybrids involving *E. ackermannii* and *E. crenatum* with species of *Heliocereus* and *Selenicereus*. There are now hundreds of named cultivars often still called Phyllocacti or Orchid cacti and frequently listed under *E. ackermannii*. The following are popular or

Epiphyllum ackermannii hybrid

Epiphyllum anguliger
hybrid

can be recommended, but a wide choice is available from specialist nurserymen; most bloom in spring:
'Autumn', coral-pink.
'King Midas', golden-yellow with darker centre and outer tepals.
'London Glory', deep red to purple, very free-flowering.

EPIPREMNUM
Araceae

Epipremnum aureum

Origin: *Tropical Asia. A genus of about ten species of climbers with aerial roots, having alternate leaves very different in young and adult stages, and arum-like flowers which are, however, not produced on pot plants. The species described is grown for its decorative foliage, particularly in its variegated forms. Propagate by cuttings and layering in warmth in summer.* Epipremnum *derives from the Greek* epi, *upon and* premnon, *a trunk, alluding to its habit in the wild of climbing up tree trunks.*

Species cultivated
E. aureum (*Pothos aureus, Scindapsus aureus, Raphidophora aurea*) Devil's ivy, Golden Pothos, Taro vine Solomon Is.
Still usually sold as *Scindapsus*, this plant owes its variety of Latin names to the fact that until 1956 it was not seen in bloom, so accurate naming was not possible. In the wild it reaches 12m (40ft) or more in height, in a pot it will seldom exceed 2m (6½ft). Leaves are oval and lobed to make a heart shape, growing to 15cm (6in) long on pot

plants, dark green with yellow marbling. *E.a.* 'Marble Queen' is more frequently met with, being less robust than the true species and having dark green leaves heavily marbled with creamy white.

FATSIA
Araliaceae

Origin: *Japan, Korea and Taiwan. A genus of one or two species of evergreen shrubs with alternate leaves shaped like outspread hands, which are dark green and conspicuously white-veined. The small whitish flowers are borne in umbels which in turn make up loose panicles. They make good house and conservatory plants though are not quite as tolerant as* × Fatshedera. *Propagate by seed in spring, by cuttings in summer or by air-layering in spring. Fatsia is a Latinized version of* fatsi, *said to be an old Japanese name for the plants.*

Fatsia japonica

Species cultivated
F. japonica (*Aralia japonica, Aralia sieboldii*) False castor-oil plant Japan, S. Korea
A large shrub or small tree in the wild, growing to 2m (6½ft) or so in a pot, with stems covered in conspicuous leaf-scars. Leaves are 20 40cm (8 16in) wide, with five to nine wavy edged lobes. Flowers are 5mm (⅛in) wide, milky-white, followed by glossy black, rounded berries. *F.j.* 'Moseri' is more compact, with larger leaves; *F.j.* 'Variegata' has leaves edged with white.

GLECHOMA
Labiatae

Origin: *Europe and Asia. A genus of ten to 12 species of creeping perennials with kidney-shaped leaves and small, mauve, two-lipped flowers. Although the species described is usually thought of as a weed, its variegated form is surprisingly decorative. Propagate by division in spring, or by cuttings in spring to autumn.* Glechoma *is from the Greek* glechon, *a name for another member of the mint family, probably pennyroyal, but chosen for this genus by Linnaeus.*

Glechoma hederacea
'Variegata'

Species cultivated
G. hederacea Ground ivy
A prostrate plant, rooting at the leaf nodes. Leaves are 1–3cm (⅜–1¼in) wide, rounded to broadly oval with two lobes making a heart shape. They are hairy with shallowly toothed edges. Flowers are 1.5–2cm (⅝–¾in) long, mauve-blue and borne in whorls in the axils of the opposite pairs of leaves. *G.h.* 'Variegata' has the leaves splashed with white. Hardy.

Graptophyllum pictum

GRAPTOPHYLLUM
Acanthaceae

Origin: *Australia and Pacific islands, perhaps also West Africa, but also widely cultivated. A genus of ten species of evergreen shrubs with opposite, usually smooth-edged and colourful leaves. They have tubular flowers opening widely at the mouth, generally in shades of red and purple. The species described below is a useful house and conservatory plant. Propagate by cuttings in late spring and summer.* Graptophyllum *derives from the Greek* graptos, *to write or paint and* phyllum, *a leaf, from the patterning on the leaves.*

Species cultivated
G. pictum Caricature plant New Guinea
Reaching up to 2m (6½ft) in the wild, but less than 1m (3ft) in a pot. Leaves are elliptic to oval, growing to 15cm (6in) long, green or purplish, marked with yellow splashes and pinkish along the main vein and stalk. Flowers are tubular, 4cm (1½in) long, red to purple, growing in short spikes at the ends of the stems.

HEDERA
Araliaceae
Ivies

Origin: *Europe to the Caucasus, Himalaya and Japan; also Canary Is. and Madeira. A genus of about five species of evergreen climbers; 15 species according to some botanists. They have juvenile stems which climb by short clinging roots, and have attractive, rounded leaves*

lobed like an outspread palm. The mature phase has erect stems with unlobed leaves and is fertile, bearing small, five-petalled, greenish-yellow flowers in umbels borne at the ends of the stems. These are followed by black berries. They make very good pot or hanging basket plants, the small-leaved cultivars being particularly effective. Propagate by cuttings from spring to autumn, those taken from non-climbing stems producing the bushy, so-called tree ivies. Hedera is the Latin name for ivy.

Species cultivated

H. helix Common/English ivy Europe to the Caucasus
Leaves are 3–10cm (1¼–4in) wide, broadly oval, with three to five lobes, dark glossy green on fertile stems. This species produces a very variable range of foliage forms, among which are some of the best ivies for the home, all very shade tolerant.

Hedera helix 'Parsley Crested'

HEDYCHIUM

Zingiberaceae

Origin: *Malaysia, S.W. China to India; also Malagasy. A genus of 50 species of clump-forming perennials that grow from rhizomes, with erect, unbranched, rather bamboo-like stems. The lance-shaped, smooth-edged leaves are borne in two ranks and the narrowly tubular flowers are in spikes borne at the ends of the stems. Each flower has a conspicuous petal-like lip, which is formed from an enlarged stamen. They are best in a conservatory and are suitable only for a large room when in bloom. Propagate by division in spring.* Hedychium *derives from the Greek* hedys, *sweet and* chion, *snow, the first described species having pure white, fragrant flowers.*

Species cultivated

H. coronarium Garland flower, Butterfly ginger lily Tropical Asia, naturalized in tropical America
Growing to a height of about 2m (6½ft), often less in containers. Leaves are oblong lance-shaped, 45–60cm (1½–2ft) in length, slender-pointed, downy beneath. Flower spikes are up to 20–30cm (8–12in) long, composed of four to six comparatively large, white, fragrant blooms; each flower has a 4–8cm (1½–3in) long tube, a broad 5cm (2in) long staminodal lip and three narrower petal-like lobes. The flowering season extends from late spring to autumn. Temperate to tropical.

H. gardnerianum Kahili ginger N. India
Reaching up to 2m (6½ft) tall with leaves 40cm (16in) long by 13cm (5in) wide. Flowers are 5cm (2in) long, pale yellow, growing in spikes to 35cm (14in) or more in length, opening from summer to autumn. Cool.

Hedychium gardnerianum

Hoffmannia ghiesbreghtii
'Variegata'

HOFFMANNIA
Rubiaceae

Origin: *Mexico to northern Argentina. A genus of 100 species of shrubs and perennials some of which are grown for their handsome foliage. They have opposite pairs of prominently veined leaves and rather insignificant four-, rarely five-petalled flowers in small axillary clusters. Hoffmannias are excellent foliage plants for the warm conservatory and worth trying in the home at least in the short term. Propagate by cuttings in summer.* Hoffmannia *commemorates George Franz Hoffmann (1761–1826), a Dutch Professor of Botany in turn at both Gottingen and Moscow.*

Species cultivated
H. ghiesbreghtii Southern Mexico and Guatemala
A shrub eventually growing to 1.2m (4ft) in height, but easily grown to half this in pots. Stems are four-angled or winged; leaves are oblong lance-shaped, up to 30cm (1ft) long, deep velvety bronze-green above with silvery or pink veins, red beneath. Flowers are yellowish almost hidden by the leaves. *H.g.* 'Variegata' has leaves irregularly marked pink and cream.

KAEMPFERIA
Zingiberaceae

Origin: *Tropical Africa and S.E. Asia. A genus of 70 species of perennials growing from rhizomes and tubers, cultivated for both their foliage and flowers. The thick fleshy rhizomes are aromatic and give forth clumps of undivided, arching leaves and somewhat orchid-like flowers. The latter have three true petals and an equally large or larger staminodal lip or labellum. Needing a humid atmosphere, kaempferias thrive best in the warm conservatory, but may be brought into the home for short periods. Propagate by division in*

Kaempferia pulchra

late spring. Kaempferia *honours Engelbert Kaempfer (1651–1716), a German doctor and botanist who travelled widely in the East.*

Species cultivated

K. pulchra Thailand, Malaysia
Leaves grow one or two per shoot, spreading horizontally, broadly oval, up to 13cm (5in) long, quilted, dark bronze-green with a broken grey zone midway between the edges and the midrib. Flowers are 4cm (1½in) wide, light purple, the lip spotted white with yellow at the base, borne in summer.

LAPAGERIA

Philesiaceae (Liliaceae)

Origin: Central Chile. A genus of one species found in woods and thickets; a semi-woody evergreen climber with handsome foliage and uniquely beautiful flowers. It is the national flower of Chile, where it is called copihue. *A very rewarding plant for a conservatory or large room. After flowering, edible, yellow-green, oblong fruits may develop, the seeds of which provide a ready means of increase. These should be soaked for two days before sowing.* Lapageria *was named for Napoleon's Empress, Josephine de la Pagerie, who was a very keen gardener.*

Lapageria rosea 'Nashcourt'

Species cultivated

L. rosea Chilean bell flower
Stems twine to 3m (10ft) or more, with leaves growing 8–14cm (3–5½in) long, alternate, oval to lance-shaped, leathery and deep glossy green. Flowers are bell-shaped, up to 7cm (2¾in) long with six waxy-textured petals, rose-pink, faintly spotted within, opening in summer and autumn. *L.r. albiflora* has white flowers; 'Nashcourt' has clear pink flowers. Other forms with larger, darker, or striped flowers are sometimes available.

Ligularia tussilaginea
'Aureo-maculata'

LIGULARIA
Compositae

Origin: *Temperate Europe and Asia. A genus of 80 to 150 species of perennials most of which are deciduous, but the one described below is, however, evergreen. Unlike most of the other species it is not hardy, but makes a bold foliage plant for a large container, or can be planted out in the conservatory border.* Ligularia *derives from the Latin* ligula, *a strap, with reference to the shape of the ray florets of the daisy flowers.*

Species cultivated

L. tussilaginea (*Senecio kaempferi, Farfugium grande, F. japonicum*) China, Korea, Japan, Taiwan

A clump-forming plant, growing to 90–120cm (3–4ft) across when planted out, but can be kept in 25cm (10in) pots if regularly divided. Leaves are almost circular with faceted or very shallowly lobed edges up to 30cm (1ft) wide, thick-textured, rich glossy green. Flower heads are like 4–6cm (2–2½in) wide yellow daisies in a loose corymbose cluster above the leaves in autumn. In cultivation the normal green-leaved species is seldom seen, its place being taken by the following cultivars: *L.t.* 'Argentea' ('Albovariegata', 'Variegata'), with leaves irregularly edged and divided into segments with creamy-white and grey; 'Aureo-maculata', popularly known as Leopard plant, with leaves bearing a scattering of large, round, yellow blotches; and 'Crispata', green with a parsley-like frill around the leaf edges.

LIRIOPE
Liliaceae
Lily-turfs

Origin: *China, Japan and Vietnam. A genus of five or six species of evergreen perennials with very narrow, leathery leaves, six-tepalled flowers in racemes and berry-like black fruits. They make attractive*

pot plants. Propagate by division in spring or by seed when ripe. Liriope *was named after the wood nymph of Greek mythology who was the mother of Narcissus.*

Species cultivated

L. muscari (*L. graminifolia densiflora, L. platyphylla*) China, Japan A clump-forming plant, usually densely so. Leaves are 40–60cm (16–24in) long, strap-like, slightly arching and deep green. Racemes are level with and just above the leaves, long and dense; flowers are somewhat bell-shaped growing to 1cm (⅜in) wide, violet-purple, appearing in late summer to autumn. It is the most decorative species for pot culture and very shade tolerant. Among cultivars, 'Big Blue', 'Blue Spire' and 'Majestic' are all bigger and finer, the last two with the racemes more or less crested at the tips. 'Variegata' has the leaves with cream edges; 'Gold Banded' is similar, but with narrow yellow edges to its leaves; and 'Munroe White' has white flowers.

L. platyphylla See *L. muscari.*

Liriope muscari

MACROPIPER

Piperaceae

Origin: *Polynesia to New Guinea and New Zealand. A genus of possibly six species of evergreen shrubs formerly included in the climbing genus* Piper. *One species is cultivated and deserves to be tried more often as a foliage houseplant. Propagate by seed in spring or by cuttings in summer. Macropiper derives from the Greek macros, large, and the allied genus* Piper. *In the wild they are robust shrubs with largish leaves in contrast to the slender climbing habit of* Piper.

Species cultivated

M. excelsum New Zealand, adjacent islands In the wild, this species ranges from a small to large shrub or even a small tree; as a pot plant, it can be grown to almost any size by pruning or regular propagation. Leaves are aromatic, broadly oval

Macropiper excelsum

to almost disc-like, lobed at the base to make a heart shape, pointed-tipped, usually deep lustrous green, 6–12cm (2½–4¾in) long. Flowers are minute, forming in slender, unisexual spikes 2–8cm (¾–3in) in length.

MICROSORIUM
Polypodiaceae

Origin: *Old World tropics. A genus of about 60 species of evergreen ferns related to, and formerly included in,* Polypodium. *In the wild they are mainly epiphytic (that is, they grow perched on trees), usually with far-creeping rhizomes and undivided and pinnately lobed leaves. The species described below combine well with a collection of bromeliads or orchids, either on sections of bark or in hanging baskets. Propagate by division or by spores in spring.* Microsorium *derives from the Greek* micros, small *and* soros, *a heap, an oblique reference to the small clusters of sporangia.*

Species cultivated

M. diversifolium (*Phymatodes diversifolium*) Australasia

With rhizomes eventually reaching to several metres (yards) in length, branching, somewhat blue-green but covered with dark brown scales up to 1cm (⅜in) long. Fronds have stalks 5–20cm (2–8in) long, the blades are of three forms – undivided, smooth-edged, lance-shaped to elliptic-oblong – more or less lobed, usually rather irregularly; or regularly and closely pinnately lobed. These leaf blade forms also vary greatly, ranging from 10 to 40cm (4 to 16in), all being leathery-textured, dark glossy green. Withstands cool conditions and can be used as ground cover in the conservatory.

M. scolopendrium (*Phymatodes scolopendria*)

Rhizomes grow to several metres (yards) in time, fleshy at first then almost woody. Fronds with stalks 4–20cm (1½–8in) long. Blades

Microsorium scolopendrium

reach up to 60cm (2ft) in length, are undivided and oblong-lance-shaped or, more usually, deeply pinnately lobed, leathery-textured, deep lustrous green.

MIKANIA
Compositae

Origin: *Tropical America, West Indies, South Africa. A genus of about 250 species of mainly climbers and shrubs with a few erect perennials. One climbing species has become a popular houseplant. Propagate by cuttings or layering in summer.* Mikania *honours Joseph Gottfried Mikan (1783–1814), Professor of Botany at Prague, or possibly his son Johann Christian, who collected plants in Brazil and followed his father as a Professor at Prague.*

Mikania ternata

Species cultivated

M. ternata (*M. apiifolia*) Brazil
Stems are scrambling, and will reach up to 2m (6½ft) or much more if planted out, purple-woolly when young. Leaves grow in opposite pairs, hairy, composed of five stalked, diamond-shaped to broadly oval, lobed and waved leaflets 1.5–4cm (⅝–1½in) long which radiate out from the top of the stalk, deep purple beneath, purple-green above. This describes the foliage of the form commonly cultivated, but in the wild this is a variable species as regards leaflet numbers (three to seven) and shape and intensity of the purple colouring. Flowers are small, groundsel-like, yellowish, growing in loose corymbs in summer.

MITRARIA
Gesneriaceae

Origin. *S. Chile. A genus of one species, an evergreen climbing shrub. It is suitable for the conservatory, where it is best trained on canes or against the back wall, or for the home. It can also be grown in a hanging basket if there is room for its long trailing stems. Propagate by cuttings of non-flowering shoots in summer, or by division of large plants in spring.* Mitraria *derives from the Greek* mitra, *a cap or mitre, alluding to the shape of the seed capsules.*

Mitraria coccinea

Species cultivated

M. coccinea
A semi-trailing species with stems climbing and holding on by means of small roots; the stems can be to 2m (6½ft) long. Leaves are 1–2cm (⅜–¾in) long, oval, coarsely toothed and glossy green, borne in opposite pairs. Flowers grow up to 3cm (1¼in) long, tubular, slightly

inflated with five small, spreading lobes at the mouth, bright scarlet; they are hanging and borne one to a stem from the upper leaf axils from early summer to autumn.

NANDINA

Nandinaceae (Berberidaceae)

Origin: *India and China. A genus of only one species; an evergreen shrub grown for its decorative foliage, graceful flowers and colourful fruits. It is best in a conservatory, but can be grown in the home. Propagate by seed when ripe or by heel cuttings with bottom heat in summer.* Nandina *is a Latinized form of the plant's Japanese common name,* nanten.

Species cultivated

N. domestica Heavenly bamboo, Sacred bamboo
A slender, erect shrub with few branches, and growing up to 2m (6½ft) high. Leaves are 30–45cm (1–1½ft) long, alternate, bi- to tripinnate with lance-shaped leaflets 3–7cm (1¼–2¾in) long; they are a coppery-red in the spring, becoming green, then tinted red to purple in the autumn. Flowers are up to 6mm (¼in) long, made up of several whorls of tepals, the outer ones petal-like; they are borne in large panicles 20–35cm (8–14in) long at the ends of the stems in summer and are followed by globular, two-seeded red berries. *N.d.* 'Alba' has white fruits. Dwarf and purple-fruited cultivars have been named in Japan.

Nandina domestica

Neoregelia carolinae 'Tricolor'

NEOREGELIA
Bromeliaceae

Origin: *Tropical South America, chiefly from Brazil. A genus of 52 species of perennials that in the wild grow perched on another plant (epiphytic). They are evergreen, and the broadly strap-shaped leaves grow in rosettes, their bases widening and overlapping to form a water-holding cup. After producing flowers the rosette dies, but is normally replaced by offsets. Propagate by removing offsets, or by seed. Neoregelia derives from the Greek neo, new and Regelia, an allied genus named for E. Albert von Regel (1815–1892), Director of the Imperial Botanical Garden in St. Petersburg.*

Species cultivated

N. carolinae (*Aregelia marechalii, Nidularium meyendorfii*) Brazil
Rosettes formed of 40cm (16in) long leaves which are strap-shaped, glossy green and finely spine-toothed, the inner ones red to purplish, brightest at the centre. Flowers are blue-purple and arise from bright red bracts. *N.c.* 'Tricolor' (Blushing bromeliad) has longitudinal stripes of ivory-white that become tinted with pink as they age.
N. marechalii See *N. carolinae.*
N. meyendorfii See *N. carolinae.*

NIDULARIUM
Bromeliaceae

Origin: *South America, chiefly Brazil. A genus of 22 species of rosette-forming perennials with strap-shaped evergreen spine- or prickle-toothed leaves, the bases of which overlap to form a water-holding cup. They are all epiphytic, that is, in the wild they grow*

Nidularium billbergioides

perched on trees. *The small flowers are clustered together and are usually borne close to the centre of the rosette, but are occasionally carried on longer stalks. They have erect, hooded tepals, a charactistic that separates them from the closely allied* Neoregelia. *Propagate by separating offsets or by seed.* Nidularium *derives from the Latin* nidus, *a nest, an allusion to the shape of the plants.*

Species cultivated

N. billbergioides Brazil
Leaves are more or less erect, sword-shaped, 20–40cm (8–16in) long, bright green and shortly spiny-toothed. The flowering stem is erect, up to 25cm (10in) in height, bearing scattered, sheathing bracts and topped by a cluster of triangular oval, yellow floral bracts with greenish flared tips; flowers are 2cm (¾in) long, white.

N. × chantrieri (*N. fulgens* × *N. innocentii*)
Much resembles a finer version of *N. fulgens* with white flowers.

N. fulgens (*N. pictum, Guzmania picta*) Blushing bromeliad Brazil
Leaves grow to 30cm (1ft) long by 4.5cm (1¾in) broad, the edges coarsely spine-toothed, shining pale green with darker mottling. Flowers are blue, surrounded by bright scarlet bract-leaves in the centre of the rosette.

N. innocentii (*N. "amazonicum"*) Bird's nest bromeliad Brazil
Leaves grow to 30cm (1ft) long by 5cm (2in) broad, with finely spine-toothed edges, shining deep purple above with a metallic lustre, red-purple beneath. Flowers are white in a dense head surrounded by pink to brick-red bracts. *N.i.* 'Lineatum' has green leaves striped with many white lines, bracts are red-tipped; 'Striatum' is similar but with fewer broader white lines and red-purple bracts.

N. meyendorfii See *Neoregelia carolinae.*

N. pictum See *N. fulgens.*

OPHIOPOGON

Liliaceae
Lily-turf

Origin: *S.E. Asia from the Himalaya to Japan and the Philippines. A genus of ten or more species of tufted evergreen perennials spreading by stolons or rhizomes. Their leathery leaves are grassy in shape. Racemes of small, nodding, bell-shaped flowers are followed by berry-like seeds. Propagate by division or by seed sown when ripe.* Ophiopogon *derives from the Greek* ophis, *snake and* pogon, *beard, from the Japanese name* ja-no-hige, *meaning a snake's beard.*

Species cultivated

O. jaburan (*Mondo jaburan*) White lily-turf Japan
A tufted to clump-forming plant. Leaves are 45cm (1½ft) or more

Ophiopogon jaburan 'Vittatus'

long, only 6–12mm (¼–½in) wide, dark green, erect, then arching over. Flowers are 7–8mm (¼–⅓in) long, white to lilac, carried on racemes on stems 30–50cm (12–20in) tall in summer, followed by violet-blue oblong fruits. Sometimes confused with *Liriope*, which, however, has flowers that always face outwards or up and are never nodding. *O.j.* 'Vittatus' ('Argenteo-variegatus', 'Aureo-variegatus') has leaves that are longitudinally striped with creamy-white.

PAPHIOPEDILUM

Orchidaceae
Slipper orchids

Origin: *Southern Asia from the Himalaya east to New Guinea. A genus of 50 to 60 species including both terrestrial and epiphytic orchids (that is, those that are ground dwelling and those that live perched on trees), for a long time classified in* Cypripedium, *a genus now used only for a group of frost hardy terrestrial orchids. They are without pseudobulbs, having a tufted habit and thick evergreen leaves at the base of the plant which are usually strap-shaped. Their flowers are borne singly or occasionally in racemes on long stalks. Each has an erect top tepal, two fused ones appearing as one, pointing down, two smaller, narrower lateral or wing tepals that usually curve downwards, and a pouched lip supposedly like a helmet or the toe of a slipper, hence their common name of slipper orchids. Propagate by division when re-potting.*

Species cultivated

P. bellatulum Burma, Thailand
Leaves are narrowly elliptic to tongue-shaped, about 15cm (6in) long, dark green with paler spots or mottling above, red-purple beneath.

Paphiopedilum bellatulum Flowers reach a width of about 6cm (2½in), and are white with a variable amount of red-purple spotting. Tepals are very broad and overlapping to form a rounded flower, the lip small and oval; the flowering stem is short, the flower carried on or just among the leaves in spring. Tropical.

P. insigne Himalaya

The green leaves grow up to 30cm (1ft) long, and are unmarked. Flowers are 10–13cm (4–5½in) wide, the top tepal green, waved, white at the tip, otherwise spotted and streaked with brown, wings yellow-green with brown veins, the lip green flushed with brown,

Paphiopedilum 'Brownstone'

glossy; they grow one to a stem but sometimes in pairs, on stems up to 30cm (1ft) tall, from autumn to spring. The amount of shading and spotting varies considerably and a number of forms are listed, some probably of hybrid origin. Temperate.

Hybrids

Garden origin. The greenhouse slipper orchids have long been popular among specialists and laymen alike and many hybrids have been bred. Hundreds of cultivars have been recorded, though a fairly limited number of these remain commercially available. On the whole, hybrids are a better choice as houseplants, particularly those derived from *P. × insigne*. They tend to be more vigorous and to have larger flowers than the species and generally bloom more regularly.

PELLAEA

Sinopteridaceae (Polypodiaceae)

Origin: *Temperate and sub-tropical regions with the majority of species in the Americas. A genus of 80 species of evergreen ferns, that are tufted or grow from rhizomes. They have pinnate to tripinnate fronds with small very narrow to disc-shaped pinnae. The globular to oblong spore clusters (sori) are usually close to the pinnae edges, which are rolled over to cover them. They are tolerant of more dryness than many ferns. Propagate by spores, or by division when re-potting, both in spring. Pellaea derives from the Greek* pellaios, dark, *because of the purple to black frond stalks of many species.*

Pellaea rotundifolia

Species cultivated

P. rotundifolia Button fern New Zealand, Australia and Norfolk Is. A clump-forming species with creeping rhizomes. Fronds grow to 30cm (1ft) or more in length, are arching to lying flat on the ground, the alternate pinnae are 1–2cm (⅜–¾in) long, disc-shaped to broadly oblong, 20 to 60 forming each frond; the dark stalks are covered in red-brown scales and bristly hairs.

PEPEROMIA

Piperaceae

Origin: *Tropics and sub-tropics, world-wide. A genus of about 1,000 species of small annuals and perennials, many of which are epiphytic (growing perched on trees) in the wild. They have fleshy leaves which range from lance- to disc-shaped and are often decoratively marbled or veined, with spikes of small, usually insignificant flowers. They make good foliage pot plants. Propagate by division at planting time, or by seed or cuttings of leaves or stems in spring or summer in*

warmth. Peperomia *derives from the Greek* peperi, *pepper and* homoios, *resembling, because of the likeness of some species to the related true pepper,* Piper.

Species cultivated

P. argyreia (*P. sandersii*) Water-melon begonia Tropical South America

A tufted plant, growing to a height of 15–20cm (6–8in). Leaves are 6–13cm (2½–5in) long, broadly oval with the stem seeming to grow from underneath the leaf rather than at the edge. They are dark green with silvery-grey areas between the veins.

P. caperata Emerald ripple Probably Brazil, but uncertain

A tufted plant, 10–15cm (4–6in) tall, densely covered with leaves; these are 2–5cm (¾–2in) long, broadly oval with deeply impressed veins, glossy deep green. Flowers are white, in tail-like spikes. *P.c.* 'Tricolor' has the leaves suffused and edged with pink and white.

P. fraseri (*P. resediflora*) Flowering mignonette Ecuador

A tufted plant with leaves growing up to 4.5cm (1¾in) long, broadly oval to rounded heart-shaped, the surface being deep matt green, shiny, bullate. Flowers are white, growing in 5cm (2in) long fluffy spikes on 30cm (12in) or more long, branched red stems. The only species that is grown chiefly for the attraction of its flowers.

Peperomia argyreia

Peperomia fraseri

P. magnoliifolia Desert privet West Indies, Panama and northern South America
Stems are erect and frequently branched, bending downwards when old, to 25cm (10in) or more long. Leaves are alternate, up to 10cm (4in) long, oval to rounded, firm and fleshy in texture, dark green. *P.m.* 'Variegata' has cream young leaves becoming green as they age.

PILEA

Urticaceae

Origin. *Tropics and sub-tropics world-wide. A genus of between 200 and 400 species of annuals and perennials with opposite pairs of oval leaves sometimes with decorative patterning and tiny, rather inconspicuous panicles or cymes of petalless flowers. They make excellent container plants, thriving best with extra humidity in summer. Propagate by cuttings from late spring to late summer with bottom heat.* Pilea *derives from the Latin* pileus, *a cap.*

Species cultivated

P. cadierei Aluminium plant Vietnam
A branching perennial reaching a height of 30cm (1ft). Leaves grow to

Top *Pilea involucrata* 'Norfolk'
Above *Pilea peperomioides*

7cm (2¾in) long and 5cm (2in) broad, oval, with a sharply tapered pointed tip. They are dark green and the areas between the veins are raised with a silvery-white metallic sheen. *P.c.* 'Minima' is similar, but smaller in all its parts.

P. involucrata Panamiga, Friendship plant Panama to Northern South America

Stems have prostrate stems with erect tips to ascending, 10–15cm (4–6in) tall by up to twice as wide. Leaves are 4–5cm (1½–2in) long, broadly oval, rounded-tipped, hairy, shallowly toothed, corrugated between the veins, bronze-green above, reddish below. *P.i.* 'Norfolk' has silvery-grey zones between the main leaf veins.

P. peperomioides China (Yunnan [Hunnan])

A clump- to mound-forming species, 20–30cm (8–12in) or more in height and width, formed of numerous suckers direct from the roots. Each stem is unbranched, becoming woody with age, with a tuft of foliage at the top. Leaves are broadly oval to almost rounded, with the stem seeming to grow from underneath the leaf, 6–11cm (2½–4½in) long, fleshy, bright sub-lustrous green. Flowers are greenish-yellowish, tiny, in fluffy panicles, but insignificant and often produced only in very small numbers (it seems to need a cool winter period to flower well). This description is of the material generally cultivated.

P. spruceana Peru, Bolivia

Much like *P. involucrata* and perhaps conspecific. Having oblong to oblong oval leaves with broadly pointed tips. Rarely seen in cultivation, plants under this name being *P. involucrata*.

PITCAIRNEA

Bromeliaceae

Pitcairnea maidifolia

Origin: *Tropical America with one species in West Africa* (P. feliciana). *A genus of about 250 species of evergreen, normally ground-dwelling bromeliads. They have rosettes of strap-shaped to elliptic or very narrow leaves often spiny-edged, and tubular, asymmetrical, three-petalled flowers in racemes or panicles. Propagate by division or seed in spring.* Pitcairnea *was named for William Pitcairn (1711–1791), a London physician who kept a private botanic garden at Islington.*

Species cultivated

P. integrifolia Venezuela, Trinidad

Leaves are very narrow, 60–90cm (2–3ft) long, tapering to a thread-like point, matt green above, grey-white-scaly beneath. Inflorescence is a pyramid-like panical growing to 45cm (1½ft) or more long; flowers are 3–4cm (1¼–1½in) long and bright red.

P. maidifolia Costa Rica to Colombia, Guyana and Surinam

Leaves are lance-shaped, tapering to a stalk, 45–90cm (1½–3ft) in length, green. Inflorescence is an undivided spike-like raceme

30–45cm (1–1½ft) long; flowers are green and yellow or white, 5cm (2in) or more in length, each one in the axil of a broadly oval, green or yellow bract about 3cm (1¼in) long.

PTERIS

Pteridaceae
Brake ferns

Origin: *Cosmopolitan. A genus of about 250 species of tufted to clump-forming ferns with long-stalked pinnate to bipinnate fronds. The rolled under edges of the fronds cover the spores. They make good container plants for home or conservatory. Propagate by division at potting time or by spores in spring at 18°C (66°F).*

Species cultivated

P. cretica Ribbon fern, Table fern, Cretan brake Tropics and sub-tropics
Fronds are 30–45cm (1–1½ft) long, pinnate, with five to 13 narrowly lance- to strap-shaped pinnae, 7–15cm (2¾–6in) long, the basal ones often divided into two or three lobes. Many cultivars are available including: 'Albo-Lineata', pinnae are slightly broader with a wide central whitish band; 'Childsii', pinnae lobed, waved and frilled, light green; 'Major', robust, with the lower pinnae often deeply cut; 'Major Cristata' ('Wimsettii'), fronds irregularly lobed and toothed, ends of the pinnae often crested; and 'Mayi', like a dwarf 'Albo-Lineata', with crested tips to the pinnae.

P. quadriaurita (*P. biaurita*) Tropics
A robust species with fronds growing to 60cm (2ft) long, more in the wild; they are bi- to tripinnate, the oval to lance-shaped pinnae being finely toothed. 'Argyraea' (*P. argyraea*) is the form usually grown, the pinnae having a central white band.

Left *Pteris cretica* 'Childsii'
Below *Pteris quadriaurita* var.

REINECKEA
Liliaceae

Reineckea carnea

Origin: *Japan and China. A genus of one species of grassy perennial that is suitable for the conservatory and home windowsill and also makes good ground cover for a floor-level bed. Propagate by division in spring or by seed when ripe.* Reineckea *was named for Johann Heinrich Julius Reinecke (1799–1871), a German gardener.*

Species cultivated

R. carnea (*Liriope hyacinthiflora*) Japan, China
A perennial forming dense clumps and growing from rhizomes. Leaves are 10–40cm (4–16in) long, all from ground level, very narrow to lance-shaped, very dark green. The pale pink flowers are 8–12mm (⅓–½in) long, bell-shaped, with six arching lobes bent back abruptly, in 8cm (3in) long spikes in late summer, followed by red, berry-like fruits. *R.c.* 'Variegata' has leaves with longitudinal, creamy-white stripes.

RHAPIS (RHAPHIS)
Palmae

Rhapsis excelsa

Origin: *Southern China to Java. A genus of nine to 15 species of very small clump-forming palms with bamboo-like stems. The one described below thrives in containers, making an elegant and neat foliage plant. They have erect, unbranched stems which sucker freely at the base, and leaves lobed like an outspread palm, the stalks of which are fibrous and sheath the main stem. The flowers are of single sex, yellowish, and borne in short clusters among the leaves, but they are not conspicuous. Propagate by suckers, division and seed in spring.* Rhapis *derives from the Greek* rhapis, *a needle, presumably referring to the narrow leaflets or their pointed tips.*

Species cultivated

R. excelsa Ground rattan, Bamboo/Miniature fan palm, Little lady palm Southern China
In containers this species grows to about 1.5m (5ft) in height (to twice this in the wild). Stems are covered with coarse leaf sheath fibre. Leaves are composed of three to ten lance-shaped, deep lustrous-green, somewhat puckered leaflets 20–30cm (8–12in) long. A very variable species in height and leaflet number. Long cultivated in China and Japan; in the latter country there is a society devoted to collecting and cultivating variants of this and *R. humilis*, at least a hundred of which have been named. Some of these are now in cultivation in the West. *R.e.* 'Variegata' has the leaflets striped with ivory-white.

Above Rhipsalis baccifera
Left Rhipsalsis cruciformis

RHIPSALIS
Cactaceae

Origin: *The Americas from southern USA to northern South America, with a few species in Africa and Sri Lanka, though these may be introductions. A genus of 60 species of somewhat shrubby frequently branched epiphytic cacti (that is, they grow perched on trees in the wild). They have often hanging, leafless stems, which are cylindrical or flattened and blade-like. The small, funnel-shaped flowers have few tepals and are followed by rounded, slightly sticky berries, which are often white and semi-transparent. The plants are best in hanging baskets, but can be grown in pots or pans. Propagate by cuttings in summer or by seed in spring.*

Species cultivated
R. baccifera (*R. cassutha, R. cassytha*) Mistletoe cactus Florida to Brazil and Peru, Africa, Sri Lanka
Stems are hanging, and capable of reaching 2m (6½ft) or more in length, cylindrical, light green. The greenish flowers are 6mm (¼in) across, followed by translucent whitish berries, which are 4–5mm (⅙–⅕in) wide.

R. cruciformis (*Lepismium cruciforme*) Brazil
Stems are trailing to hanging, up to 60cm (2ft) or more long; stem joints are 15 30cm (6–12in) long, three- to five-ribbed or winged, tapering towards the tips, shallowly notched with some white bristles, deep, almost glossy green. Flowers grow in clusters of one to five, 1.2cm (½in) wide, white. Fruits are almost the same width, globular, rich purplish-red.

RUMOHRA
Davalliaceae (Polypodiaceae)

Origin: *Southern hemisphere in tropical to warm temperate regions. A genus of one species of evergreen fern that grows from rhizomes, allied to, and formerly included in,* Polystichum, *but resembling a* Davallia. *Provides a durable and attractive foliage plant, being tolerant of low humidity and fluctuating temperatures. Propagate by spores or division in spring.* Rumohra *is named for Dr. Carolus de Rumohr Holstein.*

Rumohra adiantiformis

Species cultivated

R. adiantiformis Leather fern

Rhizomes are far creeping and densely clad in pale brown oval scales. Fronds are 60–120cm (2–4ft) or more long including the long stalks; the frond blades are egg-shaped to triangular in outline, bi- or tripinnate, leathery-textured, light green; the end pinnules are oblong, bearing beneath large spore clusters (sori), each one covered with an umbrella-like membrane with shallow teeth. It can be grown terrestrially (that is, conventionally, in soil) or epiphytically in a hanging basket.

SAXIFRAGA

Saxifragaceae
Saxifrages

Origin: Northern temperate zone and South America chiefly in the mountains. A genus of about 350 species, most of which are perennials, but including a few annuals. They are mostly tufted, with rosettes of very narrow to disc-shaped leaves. The flowers are five-petalled. Those species described below are suitable for an unheated room or porch, or a cool conservatory. Propagate by seed when ripe or in spring, by division when re-potting or by plantlets in late summer.

Saxifraga derives from the Latin saxum, a rock and frago, I break, from the habit of some species, which grow in rock crevices and appear to have split the rock.

Species cultivated

S. sarmentosa See *S. stolonifera.*

S. stolonifera (*S. sarmentosa*) Mother of thousands, Strawberry geranium Eastern Asia

A mat-forming plant, spreading by slender, branching red stolons which produce plantlets. Leaves grow to 10cm (4in) across, rounded, coarsely toothed, the upper surface silvery-hairy, the lower reddish. Flowers are about 2cm (¾in) wide, white, with two petals, sometimes only one, much longer than the rest. *S.s.* 'Tricolor' has smaller leaves with white markings and an overall pink flush.

Saxifraga stolonifera 'Tricolor'

SCHEFFLERA

Araliaceae

Origin: Tropical and warm temperate areas of Asia, Australasia and the Pacific Islands. A genus of about 150 to 200 species of evergreen shrubs and trees with alternate, long-stalked leaves with radiating leaflets like an outspread palm. The small five-petalled flowers are

Schefflera arboricola
'Variegata'

grouped into umbels which together make up racemes or panicles, but are not produced on small pot-grown specimens. They are good house and conservatory plants. Propagate by seed when ripe or in spring in warmth, by cuttings with bottom heat in summer or by air layering in spring. Schefflera *was named for J. C. Scheffler, a nineteenth-century German botanist.*

Species cultivated
S. arboricola (*Heptapleurum arboricola*) S.E. Asia
Growing to 1m (3ft) or more in a pot, and becoming a large shrub in the wild. The leaves have stalks 10–15cm (4–6in) long, with seven to 16 arching, stalked leaflets, 8–15cm (3–6in) long radiating outwards, the edges slightly folded upwards with down-curving, pointed tips. This is a handsome pot plant. Tropical. *S.a.* 'Variegata' has leaves with a yellow variegation.

SELAGINELLA
Selaginellaceae

Origin: *Mainly circum-tropical, with a few species extending into temperate and Arctic zones. A genus of about 700 species of spore-bearing plants closely allied to ferns. They have prostrate, erect or climbing stems that branch freely, in some cases in one plane to produce frond-like growths. The leaves are tiny, scale-like, usually crowded and arranged in two opposite facing ranks; the sporangia appear in compact, cone-like spikes at the ends of the stems, but are more or less insignificant. Propagate by division in spring or by cuttings from spring to autumn. The species described below make charming foliage plants for the conservatory and indoor bottle gardens.* Selaginella *is the diminutive of the Latin* selago, *once used for* Lycopodium selago *(the common or fir club moss of the northern temperate zone) and chosen by Linnaeus for this genus.*

Selaginella martensii
'Variegata'

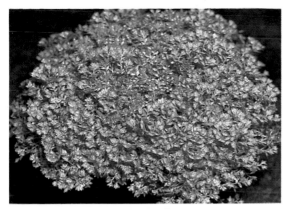

Species cultivated

S. kraussiana South Africa

A prostrate, mat-forming plant, growing up to 60cm (2ft) across, bright green, main leaves oblong lance-shaped, 3–4mm (⅛–⅙in) long. Cool. *S.k.* 'Aurea' has golden-green foliage; 'Variegata' is cream variegated; 'Brownii' forms dense mossy hummocks to 15cm (6in) across.

S. martensii Mexico

The main stems are erect, tufted to clump-forming, frequently branching above, 15–30cm (6–12in) tall in time, sprawling on and rooting into the soil. Upper branches are frond-like and ferny. Temperate A very variable species. *S.m.* 'Variegata' ('Albovariegata') has some of the branchlets splashed with white.

Above Selaginella kraussiana 'Aurea'
Above left Selaginella kraussiana 'Brownii'

SONERILA

Melastomataceae

Origin: *Tropical Asia. Depending upon the botanical authority consulted, a genus of 100 to 175 species of evergreen perennials and small shrubs. Only one species is widely cultivated for its beautifully patterned leaves and attractive flowers. It is essentially a plant for the warm humid conservatory, but responds well to being kept in a bottle garden or terrarium in the home. Propagate by cuttings in the spring or summer.* Sonerila *is the Latinized version of the native Malabar name* soneri-ila.

Sonerila margaritacea

Species cultivated

S. margaritacea Java to Burma

A tufted plant, having prostrate stems and upright tips which are reddish and branched, growing to a height of 20cm (8in) or more. Leaves are oval to lance-shaped, in opposite pairs, 5–8cm (2–3in)

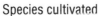

long, rich coppery-green, neatly overlaid above with a raised, pearly-silver pattern, purple-red beneath. Flowers are 1.2cm (½in) across, rosy-mauve, forming racemes. This plant is usually met with in cultivation as one of its more heavily silver-patterned leaf forms, e.g. *S.m. argentea*, 'Hendersonii', 'Marmorata' and 'Mme Baextele', the last mentioned being smaller and more compact.

STROBILANTHES

Acanthaceae

Origin: *Tropical Asia and Malagasy. A genus of about 250 species of perennials, some of which are more or less shrubby, and true shrubs. One species is grown for its highly ornamental foliage. It is best in the conservatory, but can be used in the home at least for short periods. Propagate by cuttings in spring or summer.*

Strobilanthes *derives from the Greek* strobilos, *a cone and* anthos, *a flower, referring to the bracted flower spikes of some species.*

Strobilanthes dyerianus

Species cultivated

S. dyerianus Persian shield Burma

A shrubby perennial growing to 60cm (2ft) or more in height. The stems are erect and sparingly branched. The leaves grow in opposite pairs, are narrowly oval to lance-shaped, slender-pointed and running into a winged stalk, which is up to 20cm (8in) long; the upper surface of each leaf is a blend of green, purple and silver with a shimmering iridescence, purple beneath. Flowers are 2.5–4cm (1–1½in) long, narrowly funnel-shaped with five rounded petal lobes, pale blue or lavender in short, and dense spikes at the ends of the stems. The slender-stemmed, willow-leaved cultivar 'Exotica' is probably a distinct, un-named species.

STROMANTHE

Marantaceae

Origin: *Tropical America. A genus of about a dozen species of perennials related to* Maranta *and* Calathea. *They are evergreen plants growing from rhizomes, with ornamental undivided leaves and small, three-petalled, asymmetrical flowers that are largely insignificant, but are carried in the axils of red bracts. Propagate by division in spring and summer.* Stromanthe *derives from the Greek* stroma, *a bed and* anthos, *a flower, the shape of the inflorescence.*

Species cultivated

S. sanguinea Brazil

A clump-forming plant, with stems growing to 1.5m (5ft) tall. Leaves

Stromanthe sanguinea

are elliptic-oblong to lance-shaped, 25–40cm (10–16ft) long, lustrous rich olive-green above, purple-red or striped green beneath.

SYNGONIUM
Araceae

Origin: *Tropical areas of the Americas and the West Indies. A genus of 20 species of evergreen climbers, normally epiphytic (growing perched on trees) in the wild. Their leaves vary in size and shape from juvenile to adult form, usually starting smooth-edged, or arrow-shaped, later becoming trifoliate or pedate. Flowers, which are like those of the arum, are produced only on adult plants, the spathes being white, green or purple. They make very good house or warm conservatory plants, looking their best when in a humid atmosphere but tolerating drier air. As they mature they need support for the climbing stems, a moss stick being very suitable. Propagate by cuttings of stem sections in summer. Syngonium is derived from the Greek* syn, *together and* gone, womb, *an allusion to the united ovaries*

Species cultivated

S. podophyllum Goosefoot plant, Arrowhead vine Mexico to Panama

A small and compact plant while young, later producing climbing stems to a height of 2m (6½ft) or more. Juvenile leaves are shaped like an arrowhead, often suffused or veined with silvery-white; mature leaves are trifoliate then pedate with five to nine leaflets, the central one the longest. Spathe grows to 30cm (1ft) long, whitish.

S.p. 'Albovirens' has creamy-silver bands along the veins; 'Atrovirens' is darker green suffused and veined with silver; 'Trileaf Wonder' produces trifoliate leaves when juvenile which are green with a silvery-grey vein patterning.

S.p. 'Variegatum' (*Nephthytis liberica* of gardens) has arrowhead-shaped leaves irregularly splashed with creamy white.

Syngonium wendlandii

S. wendlandii (*Nephthytis wendlandii*) Costa Rica
Juvenile leaves are arrowhead- to spear-shaped, sometimes smooth edged, velvety deep green with white veins; adult leaves are all trifoliate, the central leaflet reaching a length of 18cm (7in), dark green without the white vein patterning. Spathes are 13cm (5in) long, green outside, purplish within.

TACCA

Taccaceae

Tacca chantrieri

Origin: *Tropical America, Africa, Asia, Australia, Pacific Islands. A genus, depending upon the botanical authority, of ten or 30 species of perennials that grow from rhizomes or tubers. The species described is clump-forming with attractive basal leaves and bizarre, green to maroon umbels of six-lobed, bell-shaped flowers mixed with long thread-like organs which may be bracts or modified flower stalks. Each umbel is backed by two or more broad leaf-like bracts of a similar colour. A well-grown plant is intriguing and becomes a talking-point in the conservatory or home. Propagate by division or seed in spring.* Tacca *is derived from the Indonesian common name* taka *in Latin form.*

Species cultivated

T. chantrieri Bat flower, Cat's whiskers S.E. Asia
Growing from rhizomes, with stalked leaves, 30–45cm (1–1½ft) tall, arching, the blade broadly elliptic, corrugated and lustrous green. Umbels are composed of four bracts, which are oval with two basal lobes making a heart shape, several nodding flowers 2–3cm (¾–1¼in) long and a large number of hanging whiskers, all purple-brown to maroon, sometimes greenish.

TETRANEMA
Scrophulariaceae

Origin: *Guatemala and Mexico. A genus of two to three species of low, woody-based perennials with opposite pairs of dark green leaves and tubular, two-lipped flowers opening to five petal lobes. The species described here is a house or conservatory plant. Propagate by seed in spring in warmth, or by division.* Tetranema *derives from the Greek* tetra, *four, and* nema, *a thread, for the four stamens.*

Tetranema roseum 'Album'

Species cultivated
T. roseum (*T. mexicanum, Allophyton mexicanum*) Mexican violet/foxglove Mexico
Leaves are 7–15cm (2¾–6in) long, oval, toothed, arising from near the stem base and appearing to be almost in a rosette. Flowers are violet-purple with a paler throat and tube, the lower lip whitish; they are carried in umbel-like clusters almost throughout the year if a temperature above 13°C (55°F) is maintained. 'Album' is white.

TETRAPANAX
Araliaceae

Origin: *Southern China, Taiwan. A genus of one species of shrub closely related to, and formerly included in,* Fatsia. *It is a magnificent foliage plant for the large conservatory or room, guaranteed to*

Tetrapanax papyriferus

provide a tropical look in less than tropical temperatures. Propagate by suckers in winter or spring. Tetrapanax *derives from the Greek* tetra, *four and the allied genus* Panax, *differing in having flowers with floral parts in fours instead of fives.*

Species cultivated
T. papyriferus (*Aralia papyrifera, Fatsia papyrifera*) Rice-paper plant

A suckering shrub with robust, sparingly branched, erect stems 2–3m (6½–10ft) in height. Leaves are alternate, long-stalked, the blades reaching a width of 30–60cm (1–2ft), disc-shaped, with five to 14 broad pointed and toothed lobes each with a prominent mid-vein. Flowers are small, whitish to yellowish in spherical umbels. Fruit is a small berry. The white stem pith is the source of Chinese rice-paper. 'Album' is white.

TOLMIEA
Saxifragaceae

Origin: *Western North America. A genus of one species of low evergreen perennial which makes an excellent pot or hanging basket plant. Hardy. Propagate by division or by removing the plantlets from the leaves and rooting them as for cuttings.* Tolmiea *was named for Dr. William Fraser Tolmie (1812–1886), surgeon at the Hudson Bay Company depot at Fort Vancouver.*

Tolmiea menziesii 'Variegata'

Species cultivated
T. menziesii Pick-a-back/Piggyback plant

A clump-forming plant, growing to 40–60cm (16–24in) tall when in bloom. Leaves are long-stalked, broadly oval with two basal lobes making a heart shape. They are lobed like an outspread palm, 4–10cm (1½–4in) wide, toothed and hairy. A feature of this plant which immediately separates it from *Tiarella* is the presence of small plantlets which arise where leaf stalk and blade join; these will root when they touch the soil. Flowers are 1.2–2cm (½–¾in) long, tubular, split open along one side and with five greenish-purple, petal-like calyx lobes and four thread-like deep brown petals which are borne in slender racemes in summer. A variegated form is grown.

VIOLA
Violaceae

Origin: *Cosmopolitan, the chief centres of distribution being the north temperate zone and the Andes. A genus of 500 species of annuals, perennials and sub-shrubs of which the one species listed below is*

suitable for the conservatory or home. V. hederacea can be grown as ground cover in conservatory beds, in pans or hanging baskets; propagate by division in spring. Viola is the Latin name for a violet, perhaps originally from the Greek.

Species cultivated

V. hederacea Ivy-leaved violet S.E. Australia
A mat-forming perennial 30–60cm (1–2ft) wide, which spreads by aerial stems (stolons) that root when they touch the soil. Leaves are 2.5–4cm (1–1½in) wide, kidney-shaped and light green. Flowers grow up to 2cm (¾in) wide, a typical violet but with broader petals, the upper two the largest, white with the inner third dark purple, opening chiefly in spring, but producing some flowers throughout the year.

Viola hederacea

WOODWARDIA
Blechnaceae (Polypodiaceae)

Origin: *Northern hemisphere. A genus of about 12 species of ferns with erect or creeping rhizomes from which the fronds arise. They are pinnately lobed or bipinnate and carry their sporangia in rows or chains parallel to their central veins, hence their common name of 'chain fern'. Handsome ferns for an unheated conservatory or room, tolerating cold and shade. Propagate by division in spring.* Woodwardia *was named for Thomas Jenkinson Woodward (1745–1820), a British botanist.*

Species cultivated

W. radicans Southern Europe to Canary Islands
Growing from robust rhizomes, eventually forming wide clumps. Fronds are 1–2m (3–6½ft) long, bipinnatifid, the blade triangular to

Woodwardia radicans

oval and lance-shaped in outline. The main pinnae grow to 30cm (1ft) in length, broadly lance-shaped to narrowly oval, pinnately lobed almost to the base, each lobe finely toothed and curving gently forwards. At the frond tips large bulbils (buds or gemmae) are borne, and if pegged down to the soil they will soon root and grow into young plants. Cool.

XANTHOSMA

Araceae

Origin: *Mexico, tropical America including the West Indies. A genus of 40 to 45 species of perennials growing from tubers or rhizomes, resembling* Alocasia *and* Colocasia. *Several are grown in the tropics for their edible tubers and leaves. The species described below makes a handsome container plant, having usually arrow- to spearhead-shaped leaves on long stalks from ground level and typically arum-like spathes bearing separate zones of tiny petalless male and female flowers. Propagate by division in spring or early summer or when repotting.* Xanthosma *derives from the Greek* xanthos, *yellow and* soma, *a body, referring to the inner tissues of the tubers and rhizomes of some species.*

Species cultivated

X. lindenii Indian kale Colombia
A tuberous-rooted species. Leaf blades are arrow-shaped, growing up to 30cm (1ft) in length, deep green with a bold pattern of broad white veins. Spathes are about 13cm (5in) long, green and white.

Xanthosma lindenii

GLOSSARY

Alternate One leaf at each node in a staggered formation up the stem.

Anther The male part of a flower usually consisting of two lobes or 'sacs' containing pollen grains. *See* Stamen.

Areole A tiny hump-like organ found in all true members of the cactus family (*Cactaceae*), which bears bristles, spines, hairs or wool. It arises in what is technically a leaf axil, and is considered to be a highly modified shoot.

Aril An extra external coating around a seed, often fleshy and brightly coloured.

Axillary Growing from the point where a leaf or bract joins the stem.

Bipinnate Of leaves, bracts and stipules that are doubly pinnate, i.e. with leaf lobes that are again pinnate.

Bipinnatisect Of leaves, bracts or stipules that are doubly pinnatisect, i.e. with leaf lobes that are again lobed.

Bract A modified leaf usually associated with an inflorescence, in the axils of which flowers arise. Some bracts are scale-like and insignificant, others are large and coloured.

Bullate Puckered or appearing as if blistered; used of leaves where the tissue between the veins is raised up.

Bulbil Tiny bulbs or compact immature plantlets borne above ground, mainly on the stems of lilies and on the leaves of some other plants.

Calyx The whorl of sepals that protects the flower while in the bud stage.

Capsule A dry, often box-like fruit containing many seeds and opening by pores or slits, or explosively.

Channelled Used of a narrow leaf or leaflet with up turned edges forming a channel or gutter-shape.

Cone A spike-like structure or strobilus which bears seeds (conifers) or spores (club mosses).

Corm An underground storage organ derived from a stem base.

Corolla The petals of a flower that may be separate or fused to form a funnel, trumpet or bell.

Corymb A racemose flower cluster with the stalks of the lower flowers longer than the upper ones creating a flattened or domed head.

Cultivar Short for cultivated variety and referring to a particular variant of a species or hybrid maintained in cultivation by vegetative propagation or carefully controlled seed production. Such a plant may be purposefully bred by man, or arise spontaneously as a mutation.

Cyme A compound inflorescence made up of repeated lateral branching. In the monochasial cyme each branch ends in a flower bud and one lateral branch. In the dichasial cyme each branch ends in a bud and two opposite branches.

Decumbent Having prostrate stems with the tips erect.

Digitate A compound palmate leaf (like an outspread hand) with the leaflets radiating from the top of the stalk.

Dimorphic Having two forms, e.g. some plants have two distinct types of flowers or leaves on the same plant, others have a different habit when young and adult.

Drupe A fleshy fruit, usually with one central seed.

Elliptic Usually of leaves that are broadest in the middle and taper evenly to the base and tip.

Epiphyte A plant that perches upon another, as orchids and bromeliads grow on trees. They are not parasitic, gaining moisture from rain and air, and food from humus-filled bark crevices.

Floret Tiny flowers, usually when aggregated to form larger ones as in a daisy.

Frond An alternative name for the leaf of a fern or palm.

Genus A category or classification of all living things that groups together all species with characters in common. Of the two basic scientific names which most plants have, the first is the generic, the second the species.

Glochid Tiny barbed bristle on the areole of some cacti.

Habit The general or overall appearance of a plant, e.g. erect, bushy, mat-forming, etc.

Inflorescence The part of a plant that bears the flowers consisting of one or more blooms and their leafstalks and pedicels (the stalk of an individual flower). *See also* Corymb, Cyme, Panicle, Raceme, and Umbel.

Internode The length of stem between two nodes.

Keel The two lower petals of a pea flower (members of the *Leguminosae*), which are pressed together around the pistil and stamens.

Lip The colloquial name for the labellum, the lowest of the three petals in the orchid flower. It is modified in a wide variety of ways to aid pollination by insects.

Lobe A section of a leaf, bract, etc., that is partially separated from the main part of the organ like a cape or isthmus. It is used also for the petal-like divisions at the mouth of a tubular flower.

Monocarpic Of plants that flower and seed once then die. Technically, annuals and biennials are monocarpic, but horticulturally the term is used for plants that live more than two years before flowering.

Mucronate Leaves, bracts, sepals or petals that narrow abruptly at the apex, terminating in a firm, often sharp point.

Nectary A small gland, which secretes a sugary liquid (nectar). Nectaries are found mainly in flowers but sometimes elsewhere such as on leaf stalks.

Node That part of a stem where the leaf is joined and a lateral shoot grows out.

Offset Botanically, a special condensed shoot borne at the end of a short stem from the base of a plant. Horticulturally, also, used of any approximately basal shoot that can easily be detached for propagation purposes. Also used of the small, or daughter, bulbs that form beside the main one.

Opposite Of leaves or other organs borne in pairs on opposite sides of a stem.

Panicle An inflorescence of several racemes or cymes.

Pappus In general, the tuft of hairs on a seed or fruit to assist distribution by wind.

Pectinate Like the teeth of a comb; used of pinnate leaves, bracts or sepals with many narrow leaflets or lobes at right angles to the midrib. Also of leaves, bracts or petals with a fringe of coarse hairs.

Pedate A palmatisect leaf (rounded and palmately lobed almost to the base) with at least two basal lobes again lobed.

Perianth The two outer whorls (calyx and corolla or sepals and petals) that first protect and then display the generative parts. In a general way perianth is used when the petals and sepals look alike as in a tulip.

Pinnate Of a leaf composed of two ranks of leaflets on either side of the midrib.

Pinnatifid A leaf divided pinnately to half up the midrib.

Pseudobulb A swollen aerial stem typical of epiphytic orchids.

Procumbent Lying flat on the ground; in the strict sense, of stems that do not root as they grow.

Raceme An inflorescence composed of a central or main stem bearing stalked blooms at intervals.

Receptacle The usually enlarged stem tip, which bears the floral whorls (petals, sepals, etc.); also the greatly flattened stem tip which bears the florets of daisy or scabious bloom.

Rhizome A more or less underground stem that produces roots and aerial stems. In some cases they are slender and fast growing, in others fleshy with storage tissue and then elongating slowly.

Rootstock Botanically an approximately erect rhizome as found in some ferns. Horticulturally used for the ground-level junction of a compact perennial plant from which roots and leaves or stems arise. Also a horticultural term for a plant or its root system upon which another is grafted.

Scape A leafless flowering stem which arises direct from ground level, e.g. a daffodil.

Sepal The outer whorl of the perianth of a flower, usually green but sometimes coloured and then petal-like.

Spadix A thick fleshy flower spike with the small flowers embedded in pits or sitting flush with the surface; typical of arum lilies and other members of the *Araceae*.

Spathe A green or coloured petal-like bract, which surrounds or encloses the spadix, q.v.

Species A group of individual plants which breed together and have the same constant and distinctive characters, though small differences may occur.

Spore Minute reproductive bodies formed of one or a few cells together, which give rise to new individuals, either directly as in fungi, or indirectly as in ferns.

Sporangium An asexually formed spore.

Stamen The male unit of a flower comprising two anther lobes joined together at the top of a filament (stalk).

Staminode A rudimentary stamen, sometimes functioning as a petal or nectary, but usually producing no viable pollen.

Standard The upper or top petal of a pea flower, or the three inner usually upstanding petals of an iris bloom. Also a gardening term for a tree-like plant with an unbranched main stem and a head of branches.

Style The stalk that joins the pistil to the stigma.

Subshrub A small shrub that is woody at the base only, the upper part, particularly flowering stems, dying back each winter. From a gardening point of view the term is also used loosely for any low-growing softish-stemmed shrub.

Subspecies A distinct, true breeding form of a species, often isolated geographically from the species itself and differing more significantly than a variety.

Syncarp An ovary (later a seed pod or fruit) formed by the fusion of several carpels, e.g. lily, poppy, pineapple.

Tepal Used of petals and sepals combined when they look exactly alike, e.g. tulip, crocus, narcissus.

Trifoliate Mainly of leaves divided into three leaflets, but sometimes used for whorls or groups of three leaves.

Tuber Usually underground storage organs derived from stems and roots. Root tubers, e.g. dahlia, do not produce buds, new growth arising from the base of the existing or old stems. Stem tubers, e.g. potato, bear buds (the eyes of a potato) of which some form the next season's stems.

Tubercle A small wart or knob-like projection on a stem, leaf, or fruit, etc.

Umbel An inflorescence of stalked flowers all of which arise and radiate from the tip of the main stem.

Unifoliate Of plants with one leaf only. Also used of compound leaves (usually pinnate or trifoliate) that are reduced to one large leaflet only.

Variegated The white to cream or yellow markings on leaves due to lack of chlorophyll. Sometimes there are also tints of red, pink or purple. There are three primary causes: mutation, virus infection and a deficiency of an essential mineral which upsets the formation of chlorophyll.

Whorl Of leaves, bracts or flowers arranged in a ring of three or more.